D1395575

WRITERS OF THE DAY

GENERAL EDITOR BERTRAM CHRISTIAN

ARNOLD BENNETT

By F. J. HARVEY DARTON

ARNOLD BENNETT

ARNOLD BENNETT

By

F. J. HARVEY DARTON

NEW AND REVISED EDITION

London

NISBET & CO. LTD
22 BERNERS STREET, W.

"Nobody at all is quite in a position to choose with certainty among modern works. To sift the wheat from the chaff is a process that takes an exceedingly long time. Modern works have to pass before the bar of the taste of successive generations."

ARNOLD BENNETT,
Literary Taste, chap. vi.

Printed in Great Britain
by The Riverside Press Limited
Edinburgh

CONTENTS

NOTE

In revising this book and adding observations on Mr Arnold Bennett's chief later works, I have corrected some minor errors of fact. But with one exception—in a note on a very recent novel—I see no reason to modify materially the opinions I held when I first wrote it. And my then severest critics have now in their very reviews adopted as faith what they formerly called heresies. Because I revere Mr Bennett's best work, I cannot be so uncritical as to praise his worst.

I should add that while an attempt has been made to combine some sort of bibliographical history with a survey of *The Truth about an Author*, the evolutionary point of view has governed my own; and that I am writing about Mr Bennett as a fluctuating artist, and not as a man.

F. J. H. D.

I

THE INDUSTRIOUS APPRENTICE

BY a custom not unusual among authors, Arnold Bennett has renounced one gift of his godparents. It may be a mere perversion of modesty; or it may be one of those practical, insidious attacks on the public memory which lead to the stereotyping of such labels as Henry Irving or Hall Caine: whatever the cause, the novelist of the Five Towns has sloughed a name. He was christened Enoch Arnold Bennett. Which noted, the first name may be left to resemble its first holder, of whom we are told that he " was not."

Arnold Bennett came into the world on 27th May 1867. On the same day of the same year was born the Card, Edward Henry Machin, and in the same year the nuptials of the Bursley old wives, Constance

7

Povey and Sophia Scales (*nées* Baines), were celebrated. This exact chronological parallel between creator and created is hardly of profound significance, but it is one of a number of minor coincidences of the kind.

" The town which had the foresight to bear me, and which is going to be famous on that score "—a cheerful piece of mock egotism from *The Truth about an Author*— was, more strictly, the district of Shelton, north-east of Hanley, in " The Five Towns " or Potteries. It is obvious that that whole region made an indelible impression on the young Arnold Bennett. He was evidently very sensitive to early impressions, and the minuteness of the local descriptions in the Five Towns novels reflects his extraordinary boyish receptivity. He says of the Baines's shop, for instance—the scene of much of *The Old Wives' Tale*—that " in the seventies, I had lived in the actual draper's shop, and knew it as only a child could know it." He remembered also the sound of rattling saucepans when he was about two or three, and " a very long and mysterious passage that led to a pawnshop all full of black bundles." These are unexciting details, but they suggest that strange process of unconscious assimilation of environment during youth which so many authors transmute in later days into the fabric of life.

Arnold Bennett clearly discovered the solace of literature, in any real sense, after his school days were over, and it may perhaps be concluded that on the whole he received in youth little vital encouragement towards letters. It was not intended that the polite profession of writing was to furnish him with the bread and butter of life, much less the cakes and ale. Like Edwin Clayhanger, he was educated at Newcastle-under-Lyme, at the Endowed Middle School. He matriculated at London University (" that august negation of the very idea of a University ") about 1885, and thenceforth devoted himself to the study of the law, in the office of his father, a solicitor.

He left the Five Towns in 1889, and went

to London, where he entered a solicitor's office, and " combined cunning in the preparation of costs with a hundred and thirty words a minute at shorthand." He received £200 a year for these services, and it was some time before he realised that he was one of Nature's journalists, and could earn greater sums by more congenial work.

Yet the realisation might have come to him even earlier. Before he left Hanley he had been an unpaid contributor to a prominent local paper. It may have been the well-known *Staffordshire Sentinel* (the *Signal* of the novels); or it may have been an evanescent rival, like those connected with " Denry " Machin and George Cannon, the bigamous husband of Hilda Lessways. For some such journal, at any rate, he acted as local correspondent, and turned out, unfailingly, half-a-column a week of facetious and satirical comments upon the town's public and semi-public life. He tried also, during this early period, to write a short story and a serial: both failures. These experiences, no doubt, helped to give him facility, while they could hardly have afforded him room for useless vanity.

If the solicitor's office did not drive him into literature, it at any rate permitted the study of it. Arnold Bennett collected books—as a collector, not as a reader—and " simply gorged on English and French literature for the amusement I could extract from such gluttony." A chance observation by a friend, according to his own account, revealed to him that there might be an æsthetic side to art and letters: an equally fortuitous remark, a little later, suggested to him that he himself (*soi-disant*, till then, the most callous and immobile of philosophers) might possess the artistic temperament. He won a prize of twenty guineas in a journal which it is hard not to identify as *Tit-Bits*. He had a story accepted by *The Yellow Book*. The thing was done, both psychologically and in the facts of the market: he was an author, a man of letters. The date of this new birth may be put approximately at 1893.

The *Tit-Bits* prize was awarded for a compact humorous compression of that famous one-thousand-pound competition serial, Grant Allen's *What's Bred in the Bone*. The *Yellow Book* story (*A Letter Home*) now appears as the last of *Tales of the Five Towns*, with the footnote " written in 1893 " ; it appeared in print in 1895. That same year, 1893, saw the appearance of a work at once less ambitious and less loudly proclaimed—a serial story in the children's magazine, *Chatterbox*, called *Sidney Yorke's Friend*.

His activity soon became multifarious and incessant. Arnold Bennett turned free-lance journalist, contributing all manner of articles to all manner of magazines. He attained very soon a position of some security and responsibility, as sub-editor and subsequently editor of the woman's journal, *Woman* (now defunct). Before long he was a regular contributor to *The Academy*,

then passing through a St Martin's summer
of literary excellence under the editorship of
Mr Lewis Hind (inspirer also of H. G. Wells).
The mark of *The Academy* of those days
was extreme clearness and flexibility of
expression, wide knowledge, and a well-
balanced alertness of judgment.

Arnold Bennett also acted, during this
period, as a fluent and omniscient reviewer,
a dramatic critic, a playwright and a
publisher's reader. An amusing account of
these diversions appears in *The Truth about
an Author*.

These were the outward signs of the
apprentice author. The inward grace was
a very deliberate and conscious study of
what writing meant. In 1896 Arnold
Bennett resolved to keep a journal; later
he decided that he was interesting enough
to publish it.

" Already he had decided to be a successful author, and, as he viewed it, the keeping
of a journal was a most valuable part of

the apprenticeship to that career. . . . The peril he most dreaded was idleness, and the sin of thinking without writing."

The quotation is from a privately printed journal (*Things that Interested me*. Burslem, 1906); two volumes have now been published openly (1921-1923, *Things that have Interested me*). The diary-keeper resolved to write in the journal so many words a day, to improve his powers of observation ; and he kept his word. The outcome of such discipline, joined to industry, may be judged from an entry made three years later :

" Sunday, 31st Dec. 1899. This year I have written 335,340 words, grand total. 224 articles and stories, and four instalments of a serial called *The Gates of Wrath* have actually been published ; also my book of plays, *Polite Farces*. My work included six or eight short stories not yet published, also the greater part of a 55,000 word serial —*Love and Life*—for Tillotsons, and the whole draft, 80,000 words, of my Staffordshire novel, *Anna Tellwright*.[1] "

[1] Published as *Anna of the Five Towns*.

It may not be irrelevant to insist here that things always *have* interested Arnold Bennett. In many ways a shy man, he is generous in his help and appreciation of others. His kindness is the reflection of his love of life. He may not always realise that what interests him may bore other people, and he may sometimes write in a slightly weary and languid manner ; but on the whole he retains consistently his early and eager wonder at the human kaleidoscope.

The end of the century, more or less, closes this period. The books actually produced during it, apart from minor or anonymous works, and those already recorded, were *The Truth about an Author*, *Fame and Fiction* (both of which appeared in *The Academy*), *A Man from the North* (1898), *Journalism for Women* (1898 : the fruit of experiences on *Woman*), and doubtless the substance of *How to become an Author* (published in 1903). In 1900 Arnold Bennett went to live in France, remaining there nearly eight years. Many of his books were written there, at a cottage in Fontainebleau.

II

LIFE AND LETTERS

IN ten years or so, therefore, Arnold Bennett had learned the whole various routine of literary productiveness, and had "decided to be a successful author." How did he progress towards fulfilling his hopes? What was the relation, at this period of his career, between his life and his "letters"?

His first novel, *A Man from the North*, provides an index of ambition and accomplishment. It marks its author at once as a conscious, even a self-conscious, literary artist, striving after a certain objective effect. It was published by Mr John Lane in England and the United States in 1898. To an expert, that statement alone says much. The mere print and binding of the first edition say no less. The book was, in

16

fact, a product of " the eighteen-nineties"
—of that strenuous and now dim period of
deliberate artistic hypertrophy, when the
British Barbarians were smitten from the
hill-tops, when *The Yellow Book* was born
and died and *The Savoy* rose from its
ashes, itself a phœnix burnt untimely,
when Wilde and Dowson and Beardsley
were thought shocking, and Whistler not
quite respectable. How far off, and now,
indeed, how obsolete, seems that discordant
irruption into the Victorian afternoon.

A Man from the North was phenomenal.
(I trust the real sense of the word is not yet
wholly forgotten.) It was in the movement,
but most distinctly not of it. It was before
the movement, in one sense. It wore the
literary air of the newer æsthetic evolution.
It is far the most " literary " of Arnold
Bennett's books. Like *A Letter Home*, it is
written with a visible attempt at " style "
—at using words not solely as efficient,
unemotional units in a mass. But it deals
with the very class most abhorred by the

then young lions. It is the story of a young Bursley man—a relation of the Clayton Vernons, typical Five Towns aristocrats—who came to London, to a lawyer's office, tried to become an author, half fell in love with one woman, and married another (a tea-shop waitress), eventually rejecting, for the sake of his marriage, that finer artistic career for which he was perhaps not wholly fitted. It is, to a great extent, a chronicle of the impressions London and life make on a provincial who is a mixture of business ability, artistic temperament and sensuous curiosity.

Now there is the first and greatest mystery of literature in this book. One may say Arnold Bennett was affected by the taste, the advanced taste, of his day; of course he was. One may say that, like many authors, he drew upon some of his own experiences; very likely he did. One may say that having learnt, by great diligence and practice, to write, he wrote: he did so, very skilfully; as Aristotle discovered, you become good

by being good.   One may say that he read
and absorbed much French literature.   It
is all quite true.   But not one word in those
indubitable facts explains the great fact of
authorship.   They may have been the
practical, determining causes of the new
life which success in literature meant to
Arnold Bennett.   They were not the causa-
tive causes, nor the sole stimulus.   How
did the lawyer's clerk *really* become a
novelist ?

Such a question can never be answered.
No author—unless one takes quite seriously
Poe's cold-blooded, as it were posthumous,
account of the taxidermy which produced
The Raven—has yet contrived to reveal the
obscure process by which he veritably and
demonstrably puts words together in that
order which we call poetry or prose.   Arnold
Bennett tells us that one stimulus to literature he received was a friend's remark that
he was " highly strung."   " When I had
recovered from my stupefaction, I glowed
with pride."   That sentence alone is a whole

epitome of psychology. Highly-strung
pride would write self-consciously; it
would select adjectives, track the *mot juste*
to its lair in the cerebral windings, imagine
all manner of sensitive flutterings which
could only be real emotions by a pathetic
fallacy. But it must have some subject
matter, some quick or dead experience,
upon which to work. And it must somehow bridge the immense gap between conception in the brain and the execution of
those black and white marks on paper we
call words. " Consistent sensationalism,"
in the philosophic sense, " is speechless " :
every emotion is over before it can possibly
be recorded. What appears in print is a
hybrid of impressions and reflections, varying in quality and density, according to the
mood of the moment; some scientists would
say varying according to the state of the
digestion.

A Man from the North may be taken as,
on the whole, the work of " highly-strung
pride." But the subject matter was pro-

duced out of past experience—out of cold, hoarded emotions; and the actual expression was controlled by the bloodless surgery of journalism, by the skilful manipulator of words, whose business it is, above all, to make his effects properly. Those two last possessions or qualities—experience of life and experience of letters—Arnold Bennett has always retained. The pride, the emotional conceit, he was very soon to suppress from visible appearance.

The practically coeval novel, *The Gates of Wrath*, shows pride or conceit only in a wayward form—the conceit of a man of genius setting out to show that he too can do the lesser things if he so will. Nearly every well-known novelist sooner or later unbends and tries to write a sensational novel better than the hardened professors of that trade. Arnold Bennett differs from his fellows in achieving more success than most of them; though *The Gates of Wrath* was not a very happy beginning in that vein. High spirits are in it, but neither the vital strength of

experience nor the sensitiveness of " pride."
It is concerned with a plot to do away with
a very rich young man in the interests of his
beautiful wife. It is written in the proper
tremendous manner, with palpitations and
alarms innumerable. It is of no great importance. It may be remarked that it
reveals something of Arnold Bennett's
curiously minute interest in illnesses, and
introduces a method of murder—the con-
ducting of a chill to a fever patient—used
over again in *Leonora*, a few years later.

The two handbooks to journalism and the
critical essays in *Fame and Fiction* hardly
offer the same psychological riddles as the
works of fiction. Obviously, the question
of " subject and object," the emotions which
make up personality, do not enter into their
constitution at all fully. They are reasoned
judgments upon ponderable experience.
Fame and Fiction, indeed, is typical of that
side of Arnold Bennett's work—the portion
of his individuality which is entirely clear-
headed has made up its mind upon an

almost unsympathetic balance of considerations, and says what it thinks quite plainly. Yet the judgments so delivered are at bottom matters of faith, and the faith behind them is exceedingly significant. Arnold Bennett stands out, in these essays, as two persons—as a clear-headed, common-sense analyst, the highest power, in fact, of the skilled labourer; and as a convinced literary democrat.

" The average reader [he asserts] is an intelligent and reasonable being. . . . He has his worse and his better self, and there are times when he will yield to the former; but on the whole his impulses are good. . . . In every writer who earns his respect and enduring love there is some central righteousness, which is capable of being traced or explained, and at which it is impossible to sneer." (*Fame and Fiction*, p. 10.)

That amounts to belief in the " constant " of humanity—to the faith that there is a residual element of agreement in all matters of opinion : very few people can get rid of all the accidental elements, but somewhere there is a residuum. The one good thing remains as an author's solid virtue, the many excrescences of fashion or prejudice pass. Fame dies; the soul lives. That is the belief underlying these critical essays; and it is a democratic belief, divorced from faith in public school and university education, or rank, or classical tradition. It is a trust in the ultimate good sense of ordinary men. It does not preclude a distrust of their present senselessness. Arnold Bennett tries—and tried more fully in *Books and Persons* (1917)—to find out why they are senseless in regard to particular books, and where the grain of good sense lies hid.

That point of view, a dogma of democracy, is also a corollary of skilled labour. An experienced journalist knows better than anyone that humbug, pretentiousness, cheapness can only pay continuously if they disguise themselves utterly and become different things. But authors cannot change their tunes in any real sense; at least, very few can. Therefore, if they continue to be popular over a long period, there is something in their work worth consideration. A philosopher would say that no strong heresy dies until some fraction of it has become faith. A journalist would say that

" if 50,000 people buy a novel whose shortcomings render it tenth-rate, we may be sure they have not conspired to do so, and also that their apparently strange unanimity is not due to chance." (*Fame and Fiction*, p. 5.)

That is Arnold Bennett, the journalist, speaking. It is also Arnold Bennett, the son of the most profoundly democratic society in England, the Five Towns middle class.

Journalism for Women and *How to become an Author* need not detain us. If every literary aspirant would read them, publishers and editors could take six months' extra holiday every year. Superior persons may despise such guides to the Temple of Literature. The wise, even if they do not need them, can appreciate the sanity and thoroughness of the help offered. There is never any danger that aids to perfection will produce perfection.

We are left, then, with the history of these achievements, *The Truth about an Author*. It cannot be affirmed too emphatically that this *is* the truth about an author. For some reason or other—mainly, no doubt, because the memories of reviewers are apt to be young and of short range—this book on its reissue in 1914 was treated as practically a new work, though its authorship had long been an open secret. Moreover, its substance, even in 1914, appeared to horrify many readers, who were incapable of thinking that the commerce in serious printed matter could possibly be sordid. That horror was also expressed on the first appearance of the book in 1903, and earlier in serial form. I can only say, from personal experience, that no word in *The Truth about an Author* is exaggerated, and that people who write for money cannot help seeing that money is not beautiful.

The book is a model of bland lucidity. It is written and constructed with the consummate facility of experience, and as a maliciously accurate photograph of facts it cannot but afford amusement. It proves, if proof were needed, that an apparently (but not really) amorphous book like *The Old Wives' Tale* has behind it a vast accumulation of hard work. A few great authors have never done hard work—task work, that is to say, other than the desirable flow of genius. They are very few. A literary hack may look back upon the company of his dead, and take heart; for behind him, in the obscurity of their early labour, stand Shakespeare, Fielding, Johnson, Goldsmith, Thackeray and Dickens. There is no shame in learning one's business, nor yet in making fun of one's bread and butter.

Whether *The Truth about an Author* is the truth about Arnold Bennett is altogether another question. I have said that the psychology of literary effort is a probably insoluble mystery; it is as indefinable, indescribable a thing—indeed, much the same thing—as the psychology of poetry, which all poets define differently. Arnold Bennett tells the exterior facts of his evolution, and a little of the feelings and hopes which animated him. But though he has an unusual gift of getting outside his own skin, or of personal introspection, there are elements in his character which he himself can hardly examine without prejudice. He often seems to resemble his own inimitable hero, the Card [1]—a business man with the freakish, insolent inspirations of genius, but above all a Five Towns man. It is time, therefore, to consider more closely Arnold Bennett's " domicile of origin," as the phraseology of Admiralty, Divorce and Probate would call it. He deliberately chose the profession of literature; he learnt minutely the business of it; but it was

[1] See p. 84.

ultimately his environment that conditioned his progress in that profession. It is his local environment, too, that gives him a more than local importance to English literature.

In his novels, in some cases unfortunately, he never gets really far away from that provincial outlook. In one or two—in the three or four best—he transmutes it into something wider : he makes the local atmosphere part of all humanity. But he is seldom at ease outside the Five Towns. *Mr Prohack* (1922), for instance, is about a Five Townsman whom his creator chooses to label " civil servant." It is true that he is superficially like one or two well-known civil servants. But he is no more than a smug Card in soul. Hoape, in *The Pretty Lady* (1918), when he is real, is a true Pentapolitan ; the rest of the book is surface. *The Roll-Call* (1918)—one of the best of his later novels—is full of a young provincial's wonder at London and the larger world. Let us then look at these Five Towns.

III

THE FIVE TOWNS

THE Five Towns lie in the north of Staffordshire. They are the centre of the greatest pottery manufacture in the world. " You cannot drink tea out of a teacup without the aid of the Five Towns; you cannot eat a meal in decency without the aid of the Five Towns" (*The Old Wives' Tale*, p. 3). As Arnold Bennett uses the term, the five towns are Tunstall (" Turnhill "), Burslem (" Bursley "), Hanley (" Hanbridge "), Stoke-upon-Trent (" Knype "), and Longton (" Longshaw "), with Newcastle-under-Lyme (" Oldcastle ") as a sixth: " Oldcastle," indeed, is more prominent than " Longshaw." Politically, the towns and townships are differently grouped, and are no longer five. Newcastle is a borough by itself: it has been a borough for eight hundred years, and it lives upon that ancient dignity. The other fortresses of humanity are chiefly the outcome of industrialism. They are collectively named Stoke-*on*-Trent, which comprises Stoke-*upon*-Trent, Hanley, Burslem, Tunstall, Longton and Fenton, with their suburbs: this huge new borough, with a population of 235,000, was created in 1908, and began to exist officially in 1910.

The Five Towns are also the scene of iron-smelting and coal-mining. Their architecture is therefore " an architecture of ovens and chimneys," and the atmosphere " is as black as its mud . . . it burns and smokes all night, so that Longshaw has been compared to hell" (*The Old Wives' Tale*, p. 3). Terra-cotta and unlovely unseasoned brick are the materials of its buildings; few are older than the middle of the nineteenth century, and the carbon which often adds a grey dignity to a Georgian house here but accentuates ugliness.

Yet a few miles away, in tiny villages with

which Arnold Bennett, by his use of their names for other purposes in his books, is evidently familiar, lies the ordinary, unchanging country life of England. Staffordshire is one of the most English of counties, well-watered, full of trees and meadows and little hills, green and fertile, with ancient churches and bridges, and a cathedral town, Lichfield, that has a life not only gracious with the memories of its eighteenth-century dignity, but almost coeval with Christianity in England. " It has everything that England has." Quite through its length and breadth runs " the river Trent, the calm and characteristic stream of middle England," which rises three miles north of the Five Towns, on the hill described by Arnold Bennett as " famous for its religious orgies," but more sympathetically remembered in the history of English Nonconformity as Mow Cop. On the western borders lie the romantic march lands of the Dee, the Severn and the Wye ; on the north and west the Derbyshire Moors : on the south the forgotten battlefields and the strepitant modern factories of Worcestershire and Warwickshire. A man might dream a solitary life out in the contemplation of streams and moors, ten miles from Burslem.

Some of those natural phenomena are important to this critical exposition. Indeed, all details of every environment are important: it is not unworthy of remark (Arnold Bennett remarks it) that thirty miles of Watling Street run through Staffordshire: so long and fine are the threads of local life. But there is one whole section of the county which may be neglected as utterly by the critic as it is by the inhabitants of the Five Towns: the rural surroundings of that urban district. Nowhere in all Arnold Bennett's novels, nowhere in anything he records of any of his characters' minds, is the faintest trace of any love for or even any appreciation of scenery or " natural " beauty. So Lichfield and Trent, moor and meadow, may vanish from this survey like the fabric of fairyland;

there shall be no green shades nor shining orchard peace nor Sunday calm in these pages—nothing but men and women and houses, and the fires that burn in all three.

If it were true that the real people of the Potteries (outside novels) care nothing for this quiet aspect of beauty, or for the ancient and generous past of Staffordshire as a whole —if that were true, and it may or may not be true—then there would still be no immediate ground for condemning their insensibility. It is a fugitive and cloistered æsthetic that shrinks from the dust and heat of modernity. The connection between romance and the nine-fifteen is a commonplace, and, as more than one poet has shown, it is possible to give a savage beauty to the most sordid bestialities of human nature in rural districts. A Five Towns passage which discovers the splendour that may lie in grime deserves to be taken from its context:

" To the East is the wild grey-green moorland dotted with mining villages whose steeples are wreathed in smoke and fire. West and north and south are the Five Towns. . . . Here they have breathed for a thousand years; and here to-day they pant in the fever of a quickened evolution, with all their vast apparatus of mayors and aldermen and chains of office, their gas and their electricity, their swift transport, their daily paper, their religions, their fierce pleasures, their vices, their passionate sports, and their secret ideals! Bursley Town Hall is lighting its clock—the gold angel over it is no longer visible—and the clock of Hanbridge Old Church answers; far off the blue arc lamps of Knype shunting-yard flicker into being; all round the horizon, and in the deepest valley at Cauldon, the yellow fires of furnaces grow brighter in the first oncoming of the dusk. The immense congeries of streets and squares, of little houses and great halls and manufactories, of church spires and proud smoking chimneys and chapel towers, mingle together into one wondrous organism that stretches and rolls unevenly away for miles in the grimy mists of its own endless panting." (*Whom God hath Joined*, chap. i.)

Such is the aspect of the Five Towns : a pillar of smoke by day, a pillar of fire by night. What wonder that one so full of the genius of place (a spirit of new towns no less than of old haunts of peace) should see always in such a pageant " the natural, beautiful, inevitable manifestation of the indestructible Force that is within us " ?

Upon the more minute features of this vast concourse of atoms Arnold Bennett has dealt with fulness and consistency. Any Five Townsman can recognise most of the places from the descriptions in his novels.[1] In like manner, Five Townsmen can identify certain persons and events, especially in the short stories. It would not be discreet to give the actual names of the people. The important point is the fact of Arnold Bennett's fidelity to real life, or to phases of it.

He has, on the whole, followed the period as well as the place of his own life, but only a section of the Potteries' life. The people

[1] See the Note at the end of this chapter.

in the Five Towns novels belong to hardly a dozen families. Except in a few preliminary scenes here and there, they are all above the poorest class; they are the more or less prosperous tradesmen and minor professional men of a commercial centre. Equally, they never form part of the upper or ruling classes. They are the middle class, plain and immitigable.

There are two words which Arnold Bennett constantly uses about them—" mentality " and " egotism." The first is, so to speak, his index of judgment—the creator's criterion of the created. The second is a quality objectively displayed by the persons, and not involving classification or judgment at all. The mentality of Darius Clayhanger might be called low but strong, of his son Edwin high but weak; both alike are egotists. On the whole, the Five Towns mentality, in the novels, is vigorous and coarse, and their egotism constant. But if you applied either term to the middle class of other authors, you would get very poor results. There would be plenty of idiosyncrasy, but little real mentality. They would be egoists rather than egotists (a subtle but real difference—an egoist is conceited, an egotist merely self-centred). They would be surface types, collections of idioms, so to speak. The Five Townsmen are concentrated and genuine. They show little real or apparent hypocrisy. Their substance, as well as their appearance, is balanced and solid; they are enormously robust and aggressively self-respecting. They have a corporate and individual personality.

Further, as far as social values also are concerned, they are openly and avowedly middle class. They are self-satisfied as well as self-centred. They are flattered and fluttered by the intrusions of the Countess of Chell into their civic life; but they do not, on the whole, want to resemble or form a regular part of the society she frequents. In this connection the Five Towns show some of the high self-respect of the traditional English middle class, which perhaps has never really existed except in a few London merchants of about 1450.

Egotism, then, moral and social, is their predominant characteristic. It is a local condition, explained by local conditions. The Potteries refused railways at first. They had been engaged for countless generations in one single self-sufficing and prosperous craft. They preserved, therefore, without change, not merely their trade customs, but their personal manners. They were, until quite recent years, a piece of England walled off in the very heart of England. The motor and the railway have made great transformations; but until 1880 or a little later the Townsmen dwelt like the Albanians before the Turkish Revolution, who, when the Young Turks first prevailed, were observed to come from their hill fortresses, blinking, curious, armed with strange weapons, into a world, a social order, they had never seen.

I have exaggerated their actual isolation

a little. But it is a real thing, at the root of many qualities displayed by Arnold Bennett and by the people in his books. They always think themselves right, for instance. They seldom allow for any other point of view than their own. Confronted with new or alien ideals and standards, they show a prickly defensiveness very difficult to overcome. They have never had the need for gentleness or amenity. The pot-banks two or three generations ago—described with terrible force in Chapters IV. and V. of *Clayhanger*—were a ghastly battle-field, where no pity nor weakness found room to live. The Five Townsmen of 1860 to 1900, therefore, had no tradition of refinement either of spirit or of material inter-course. Instead, they had its converse, a high standard of comfort and efficiency, and the pride that goes with such a standard. Such pride never knows when it is legitimate and fine, when unseemly and ignoble.

Here the Five Towns, indeed, are upon

strong native ground. If they are re-
proached with ugliness, they could answer
that they are footmen in the army of a great
king. They march in the ranks of an age-
long civilisation. Their toil, unlovely by
the elegant standards of Mediterranean
humanity, makes the lives of other men
more endurable and often more beautiful.
English earthenware to-day (except its
finest products) may not be satisfactory
from an artistic point of view. But it
is produced by a manual skill to the per-
fecting of which innumerable generations
have gone. The civic accomplishment of
Lichfield, that other civilisation of Staffordshire, culminated in the swannery of Anna
Seward; who shall say when pottery will
cease? An ultimate and profound clash
of ideals would be raised by the cry
latent in any Five Townsman: "We made
pots and pans here before ever a stone of
Lichfield rose. We are the people of
England. You are the imitators of Greece
and Rome and Nazareth. Get you to Capri."

Finally—and here the Five Towns are linked to the greater world—the period connected with Arnold Bennett's earlier work is one about which any generalisation made firmly to-day may be friable to-morrow. He deals with the end of one urban epoch and the beginning of a new one. By 1880 —these novels celebrate chiefly the three decades from that year onwards, especially the middle one—Victorian England was no longer Victorian. The effects of the Industrial System, the Reform Acts, the Forster Education Act, and the repeal of the Corn Laws coincided about that date to produce a new England which we, its sons, can hardly yet see in perspective. Industrial life and its surroundings, sober-seeming before then, yet once, when it first rose upon the solid early Victorian foundations, apparently garish and ill-balanced, began to receive that fresh and vivid commercial quickening which we are apt to call, with some injustice to ourselves, American. Electricity rivalled steam ; municipalities grew more corpor-

ate; comfort and wealth and population
were doubled. To a man in that welter of
the new Bursley the world must have been
what Arnold Bennett says every good
journalist finds it—interesting at every
moment of life. "For the majority of
people the earth is a dull place. . . . The
most numerous exceptions are lovers and
journalists." It is a characteristic result
of his environment that a Five Townsman
should never find life dull, and should believe himself unique in his cheery faith.

Let me here recapitulate the main
elements in Arnold Bennett's character as
an artist. He is a Five Townsman—keen,
interested, exceedingly shrewd, very practical
and efficient, limited in certain directions,
rather coarse-fibred in others. He is a
trained manipulator of words. And he is
highly strung, which means that in spite
of a most efficient self-control—indeed, as
the result of it—he is always (whether he
wishes it or not) expressing some aspect of

his experience, opening some tiny window of his soul, speaking out (however faintly) some whisper of personality. You cannot be highly strung and not do so; the deeper your sensitiveness, and the more subtly you strive to hide yourself, the more truly do you yourself appear in your work—though everyone may not see you. Any doctor will tell you that the mask of a nervous patient is what betrays him. It is the same in literature. All good authors are " nervous "— though vain, dyspeptic, artistic or greathearted are usually the adjectives of diagnosis. The truth about an author will out, even when he denies it or disguises it.

NOTE ON THE TOPOGRAPHY OF THE FIVE TOWNS NOVELS

It is possible to identify in detail most of the places in the Five Towns novels. Perhaps the attributions are not always exact, any more than in the case of Thomas Hardy's Wessex: but they are at any rate *vraisemblable*, if one allows for a few little

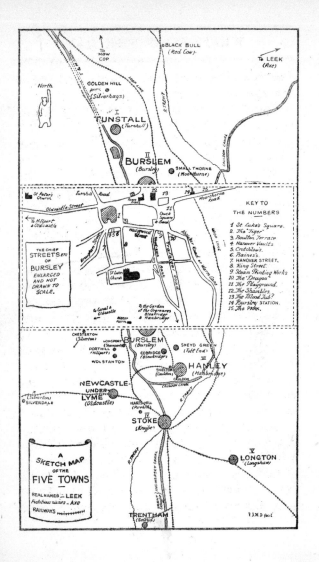

A
SKETCH MAP
OF THE
FIVE TOWNS
—
REAL NAMES – LEEK
Fictitious names – Axe
RAILWAYS ┈┈┈┈

discrepancies here and there, and local changes from time to time.

The fictitious names of the chief towns have already been mentioned. " Turnhill," " Bursley " and " Hanbridge " are those most frequently used, and of those three Bursley has the pre-eminence. In the middle of Bursley, in the market-place, stands (or stood till 1911) the Town Hall. Opposite is the Leopard Hotel (the "Tiger," famous for its barmaid). Here also is the Butcher's Market, or Shambles. The irregular space is a ganglion of streets. Eastwards runs Moorland Road (" Moorthorne Road ") to Smallthorne (" Moorthorne ") ; north of this road lies the Borough Park, and streets (" Bycars Lane " and " Park Place ") of no great importance except in *Helen with the High Hand* and *The Price of Love*. Bursley railway station is also here, and somewhere in the north-easterly region of the market-place once lay " the Blood Tub."

At the north-west corner of the market-place debouches Liverpool Road (" Turnhill Road ") ; at the west, Newcastle Street (" Oldcastle Street "). Along Oldcastle Street, past the valley in which the Trent and Mersey (" Knype and Mersey ") canal

runs, lies the route to the fashionable suburb
(really no suburb, but a separate parish) of
Wolstanton (" Hillport " and " Porthill "—
Newport, Longport and a real Porthill all
are by the way). "Shawport" Station, in
the valley, is Longport Station.

Turnhill Road and Oldcastle Street and
the end of the market-place culminate, towards the south, in the most famous of all
these haunts—St John's (" St Luke's ")
Square, where were the shops of the Baineses,
the Poveys, Mr Critchlow, Holl's, and the
office of Denry Machin. Baines's occupied
most of the south side of the Square, which,
like the north side, was split up by several
roads. South-east stretched " Brougham
Street " (which is more like Navigation Road
than anything else). From the south-east
angle Church Street (" King Street ") ran
down to the parish church of St John, and
from the same angle, almost due east, Queen
Street (" Wedgwood Street ") led to " Duck
Square " and Waterloo Road (" Trafalgar
Road "). The north-west corner of Wedgwood Street was called " Boulton Terrace ";
here Daniel Povey murdered his wife.

The Duck Square region is Swan Square
and its environs — the rather shapeless

tract between Waterloo Road proper and the market-place, with a chapel, a school, and a playground on the eastern side. At its south end (on the south side of Wedgwood Street, that is) stood the Steam Printing Works of Darius Clayhanger; Mr Duncalf's office, first scene of the Card's activities, was also in the Square.

Here again is a ganglion of roads, the chief of them Waterloo (" Trafalgar ") Road, the main trunk line between Hanbridge and Bursley. Where Trafalgar Road joined " Aboukir Road " or " Warm Lane " (Nile Street) stood the " Dragon," while exactly parallel to Trafalgar Road, for some distance, ran " Woodisun Bank."

The two Methodist chapels—Primitive and Wesleyan—are said to have been in King Street and Duck Bank respectively; but certain details here are incongruous with to-day's topography. The other Anglican Church, St Paul's (" St Peter's "), is a little distance due north-east of the market-place.

Follow now Trafalgar Road. Half-way along it, towards Hanbridge, is Cobridge, the residential suburb called " Bleakridge." Somewhere here—perhaps at the corner of Elm (" Oak ") Road—stood the new house of the Clayhangers, next to the garden of the Orgreaves, magical grove of love. To the west is George Farm ("Manor Farm"). Not far to the east of Cobridge is Sneyd Green ("Toft End"), the highest part of the Five Towns. And so to Hanbridge, whose central Square ("Crown Square"— Crown Bank is close to the Market Square) is yet another centre of traffic. But Hanbridge is nowhere so lovingly and meticulously described as Bursley; the chief features were the Saracen's Head ("Turk's Head") and Bostock's and Brunt's stores, which also have real originals. The Cauldon Iron Works are to the south: sometimes they are undisguised, but more often "Cauldon" stands for Arnold Bennett's birthplace, Shelton.

Neither is Turnhill nor Knype of much importance. At Knype is the chief railway station, where George Fearns avoided his wronged wife; at Turnhill Hilda Lessways owned some cottage property. Harts Hill ("Pirehill"), site of the chief infirmary, lies between Knype and Oldcastle. Longshaw is hardly mentioned.

A few outlying districts are brought in. "Sneyd," home of the Countess of Chell, and a Sunday resort of bloods, is obviously Trentham, till recently the Duke of Sutherland's seat. Sneyd is a famous Staffordshire family and place name. "Manifold" and "Axe," each, in the novels, situated ten miles from the Five Towns, may be meant for the same place. "Manifold" is "the metropolis of the moorlands," and that implies some town to the north or east. As a matter of fact, there is a real Manifold Valley on the east — a pleasure resort, not a town. "Axe," also on the moors, is said in *The Price of Love* to be *west* of Hanbridge; but there are no moors in that direction. Leek, about nine miles to the north-east, on the Derbyshire border, and duly "north-east of Toft End," is the most exact original of this town, from which Sophia Baines ran away to marry Gerald Scales.

East of Oldcastle are a couple of villages which provide a portmanteau name—Silverdale + Chesterton = Silverton. North of Turnhill is Goldenhill ("Silverhays"); east is Chatterley, which is not disguised. "Red Cow" should be Black Bull, a railway station north-east of Turnhill.

IV

FANTASIAS AND PHILOSOPHIES

THE classification of his writings which Arnold Bennett afterwards adopted (he was either the first modern novelist or one of the first to invent such a valuable guide to his intentions) includes six headings—Novels, Fantasias, Short Stories, Belles-Lettres, Drama and In Collaboration. The last section does not concern us much. Drama obviously requires a chapter to itself. Of the fourteen pre-war novels, ten deal almost wholly with Five Towns life, as do most of the short stories; and the later works are not confined to Staffordshire. These novels are so clearly his most characteristic production that they must be treated all together if their significance is to become plain.

We are left, then, with a collection of nondramatic, non-Staffordshire works consisting of " novels " (of which *A Man from the North* and others have been mentioned), six " fantasias " (a seventh, *The Gates of Wrath*, having been already discussed) and a number of " belles-lettres." It may seem that they form a heterogeneous crowd. As a matter of fact, they have a very distinct community of inspiration and execution. Versatile as Arnold Bennett is, he is no Proteus: there is something constant in everything he writes. All these works are different manifestations of a Five Towns democrat who was writing for a living.

Take the sensational novels first. They were not named " fantasias " fantastically. I take it that the title really conveys the author's opinion of the books. He perpetually shows devotion to music, and the word is probably, therefore, a metaphor from music. That is to say, these books are to be regarded as vivacious, skilful exercises upon certain central ideas in each case: exercises calling for high spirits, technical facility, and exuberance of ornament. They are not sonatas, operas, oratorios—not in Ercles' vein: but they are something more than frivolous improvisation—more responsible, more deliberately composed, written with a critical smile rather than a spontaneous laugh. You might say they were the handiwork of a literary "Card," showing off in a characteristically surprising manner.

That implies that there is a good deal of conscious and unconscious pretence about them. Arnold Bennett is as capable of pretence as any man. *The Truth about an Author* shows with how much serious mockery he must have enjoyed writing his first fantasia, *The Gates of Wrath*, though he called it merely a serial in those days:

" As an editor, I knew the qualities that a serial ought to possess. And I knew specially that what most serials lacked was a large, central, unifying, vivifying idea. I was very fortunate in lighting upon such an idea for my first serial. There are no original themes; probably no writer ever did invent an original theme; but my theme was a brilliant imposture of originality. It had, too, grandeur and passion, and fantasy, and it was inimical to none of the prejudices of the serial reader. In truth it was a theme worthy of much better treatment than I accorded to it."

That is the spirit of all the fantasias. They were all written for pleasure and for profit, motives indissolubly mingled. They are novels of ideas vigorously worked out, but not of great ideas. They deal each with a characteristic phenomenon of material civilisation, raised to its highest power. It must be a phenomenon plain to the average man, but not fully and gloriously realised. The author takes it, and shows every conceivable splendour of it, and some inconceivable splendours as well. He brings in, in a grandiose spirit of intensive culture, every possible illustrative ornament. He adds profuse excitement, suddenness of transition, rapidity of movement, and a worldly, caustic humour. That is the whole prescription. In spite of the novelty of conception, however, and their agile modernity, the fantasias have all a defect of execution. For obvious reasons, the *dénouement* in sensational fiction should be delayed as long as possible. Arnold Bennett postpones his revelations deftly. But he invariably overcrowds his plot and so tangles the unfolding. The striking initial incident in each case appears to be the summit of his inspiration. He lavishes great care upon it, and then does not appear to trouble so much about what follows, so long as he can pile up sensations rapidly. The result is that the reader, by the end of the book, loses the simple faith which the opening scene always inspires. It is a curious weakness for so efficient a craftsman, and suggests that the labour of fantasia-making is irksome after the first impulse is spent. This defect is practically absent from the two novels written in collaboration with Eden Phillpotts.

The Ghost is also named a fantasia, but it differs from its fellows in dealing with the spiritual world, not the very material one of hotels and motors. It tells how a masterful peer loved an opera singer so fiercely that after his death his ghost could intervene in life: he became "a malign and jealous spirit, using his spectral influences to crush the mortals bold enough to love the woman whom he had loved on earth." It is, like "the speaking marble of the soul-subduing Chiggle," a work of the Elevated or Goblin School, in which the effort to be tremendous destroys the tremendousness.

Two further works are novels of emotion. *Sacred and Profane Love* has defects very similar in origin to those of *The Ghost*, but different in manner. It is written ostensibly in the first person by a Five Towns girl who was "a secret revolutionary." After a private course of forbidden literature, she "ceased to be ashamed of anything that I honestly liked." She honestly liked voluptuousness and rather promiscuous love (" sublime immodesty and unworldliness," she called it), so that her career was at any rate unusual. Her joy was to be " a self-constituted odalisque," " a pretty, pouting plaything," " a man's woman." Only in the moment of her death is there a hint of something deeper than the merest volatile sensuality.

Both these novels really suffer from insensibility to fine feeling and fine thinking. To name other novelists who do not shrink from facts, such books could not have been written, or rather, could not have been written so, by Mr Masefield, or Mr Conrad, or Mr J. D. Beresford. I do not mean that their author lacks subtlety. Arnold Bennett is infinitely and splendidly subtle when he is working upon Five Towns material, and he is occasionally subtle also in these minor novels. But his intellect and his spirit and his literary sense alike (so far as they are revealed in his books) are inadequately tempered to fine issues. It is not unjust to the democracy of true emotion to say that

the lofty joys and victories and defeats of
the soul cannot be expressed in low words:
in words, that is, rubbed smooth or defaced
by usage. Neither can the mind triumph
coarsely, for it is not then the mind but
the animal brain answering, virtually, to a
physical stimulus.

This crudity of sexual and psychical
emotion in Arnold Bennett is emphasised
by certain points in *The Glimpse*. This, by
some aberration of the practical journalist,
was offered to *Black and White* (now dead)
as a short story. The editor justly boggled
at it, and Arnold Bennett decided it
deserved to be a novel, not a short story.
So a novel it is: the embryo is embalmed
in *The Matador of the Five Towns* under the
same title.

In *The Glimpse* all the weaknesses of the
Five Towns idealist are sadly, even patheti-
cally, manifest. It is hard to believe that,
when he wrote it, its author did not think it
a metaphysical or psychical document of
genuine value. It is equally hard not to

laugh at it. Briefly, it tells how a man of the well-to-do middle class apparently died, had a vision of the after life, and returned to this present mediocre world. It may be said at once that the three chief imaginative treatises on the same subject in modern English literature—Browning's *Epistle of Karshish*, Evelyn Underhill's *Grey World*, and H. G. Wells's short story, *Under the Knife* —are so far above *The Glimpse* that if it is to be read at all they must be forgotten. They suggest a spiritual world, a " world " in which personality, pure and simple, persists in a manner compatible with some hard struggle to conceive what personality really is. *The Glimpse* merely offers the crude metaphors of spiritualism visualised, with no added profundity of thought. Arnold Bennett is not, in matters like this, a scientist : he cannot, as H. G. Wells does, suggest the continuity of obscure "psychical" forces which would give plausibility to a bare assertion. Nor is he a metaphysician like Miss Underhill.

I am loth to dwell on such a failure as this. But I must add that it is a complete failure in detail. It contains provincialisms which make it impossible to accept the chief man and woman at their alleged London value. The " astral " scenes are written in a style of exuberant Latinity which would put a botanist to shame. The conception of woman formulated is Victorian - Turkish; and a man's sense of humour must be temporarily in abeyance when he lets himself write of a female soul-form that " the woman I had created . . . was only an ineffable extension of my egoism."

The extension of Arnold Bennett's egoism in these three very unfortunate books is an adventure upon ground unsuited to a character so trained and so temperamentally disposed. These are novels based upon emotion rather than experience, and emotion is the best of servants, the worst and least stable of masters. The peculiarity of Arnold Bennett's genius is that it is at its highest when it is most severely controlled.

Some later works have already been mentioned (see p. 29). In the same category as *The Pretty Lady* may be placed *Lilian*. But there remain two novels, on the other hand, which are marred by no ill-equipped extravagance. They are virtually fantasias in conception, but novels by their deeper reality. *Buried Alive* is a genuine comedy, written with a humorous acidity which only in one scene is remote from minute and thoughtful observation. *A Great Man* —" a frolic "—shows the same powers of comic observation, applied not only to the business side of literature but also to the psychological state of authorship. It is almost a fictitious appendix to *The Truth about an Author*.

A slight jejuneness of social observation may be mentioned here. It leads Arnold Bennett now and then to use the same details more than once. For example, he employs precisely the same image, and almost exactly the same words, in *The Honeymoon*, of Mrs Reach Haslam, the talented novelist, and in *Buried Alive*, of Priam Farll. There are several instances of the practice: perhaps the most noticeable is the employment twice over of a description of a paintress's work— in *Anna of the Five Towns* and in a short story. Of course it is no vital defect of genius. It simply suggests a certain pigeon-holedness of mind which is the danger of efficiency.

Most of the novels dealt with in this chapter are, so to speak, pastimes: experiments, efforts at self-expression, which Arnold Bennett has made concurrently with more deliberate work upon his native raw material. It must be taken as a self-evident proposition that the Five Towns novels are far higher achievements. These works are merely clever. At the same time, the "highly-strung pride" of the author crops up in them—in the *flair* for a surprising situation, the evident enjoyment of it; in the desperate earnestness of the assertion of his own beliefs—beliefs upon matters, as I have said, alien to his temperament; in

the quiet detachment of the humour. The
" Philosophies " show the processes of observation and self-training and experience
which were going on behind the experiments.
Arnold Bennett tried, in these novels, to
suit public taste—to supply a market. To
that end, he trained his mind, he learnt his
trade, he formulated his ideals (or some of
them) in very distinct words. He arrived
at a gospel of mental and moral and practical
efficiency which he had hitherto been follow-
ing without writing it down. The pocket
philosophies contain it.

They appear in England under a handicap.
Expressing the view that life is earnest, they
are labelled as though they proclaimed that
life is humbug. On their wrappers appears
the language of what used to be called
advertisement: it is now publicity. One
book, for instance, is said to contain " big,
strong, vital thinking . . . thoughts that
make a man reach up to his highest self.
For many a reader a chance encounter with
this book may be the first step on the road

to success." Somehow, successful men always claim the best of both worlds. . . . However, " big, strong, vital thinking " is just what these remarkable little books do not contain. They contain the completest common-sense, expressed with astonishing simplicity and directness, and based upon unimpeachable honesty of outlook. They are a guide to efficiency, to self-help, to practical idealism, to alertness of intelligence, to sinewy culture, to every high quality which every person who sets out to advise the crass Briton has always thought the crass Briton does not show. The United Kingdom is quick with the instinct of mind-moulding, and almost overstocked with agencies for the purpose, from the physical energies of Mr Sandow to the benevolent writings of the late Lord Avebury. Where Arnold Bennett's handbooks to *The Reasonable Life* differ from the scores of books and lectures and charts with similar aims is in economy, clearness, and comprehensiveness of language. They are quite perfect lay sermons. But they are not original.

Other aspects of his philosophy are revealed in *Paris Nights, The Log of the "Velsa,"* and *Those United States*, where he appears as what he is professedly anxious not to seem—a typical Englishman. He is detached, humorous, self-depreciating : he knows and explains how much better many foreign customs and achievements are than their counterpart in England. But he can help, no more than a *Times* leader-writer, a carefully suppressed sense of patronage.

The chief notes of travel in these two books, on the whole, are practical—concerned with manners and facilities rather than ideals. But they show, much more than, for instance, the handbooks, and more than most of the novels, how wide is their author's range of knowledge and experience. Had he chosen to write in a style of forcible allusiveness, like Mr Kipling, Arnold Bennett would be famous for his recondite technical learning. Because his method is silent, not emphatic, his curious lore seems to be merely careful photography. He has assimilated as well as catalogued.

In *Liberty, Over There,* and the fine introduction to Harold Rosher's *In the Royal Naval Air Service* he is outspokenly and obviously English—clear-headed, thorough, and passionately democratic. He served with distinction in the Government propaganda department during the war.

There is a sincerity in all his practicalness. In the war essays it is perhaps clearer because the subject is greater. But he is just as fully convinced and in earnest when he suggests hours for the reading of good literature, half-hours of concentrated thought, careful study of a particular art, and so on. When he turns his practical gifts on to the concoction of fantasias, the sincerity may seem to diminish or even to disappear: the psychology of literary composition certainly helps to obscure it. Yet it is still there, in the shape of an immense interest in civilisation—a lively inquisitiveness and keenness and self-confidence. The fervour, the bustle, the desire to do something and not to rest, which animates the Five Towns, animates Arnold Bennett. So does the Five Towns' firm conviction that all men are equal, and all entitled to life, liberty and the pursuit of happiness. So, at times, does the not-always-lofty Five Towns' conception of what happiness and life are, and their perfectly legitimate readiness to sell, as books, any views formed upon such subjects.

V

THE FIVE TOWNS NOVELS

IN the preface to a re-issue of his greatest
book, Arnold Bennett lays bare, con-
sciously and unconsciously, certain
secrets of his art. I have said that he
deliberately became a writer, and that, however deliberate a man may be, he must
reveal himself willy-nilly. This is how he
says he wrote *The Old Wives' Tale*. He
used to see, at a restaurant in Paris, a young
and pretty waitress, heedless of him, and a
less pleasing one who wanted him for her
own. They were to him, one would think,
an epitome of life. One day a plain, elderly
lady entered, and appeared, to unthinking
persons, ridiculous. The pretty waitress
laughed at her. Arnold Bennett, from
whom, for all his humour, the tears of
human things are not hidden, saw in the

absurd woman " a heart-rending novel."
She had once been young and had grown
old, had developed " from a young girl into
a stout old lady." He resolved to write that
novel. But he saw that if he wrote about
an ordinary woman, she must not (at that
epoch) be singular or ridiculous : she must
" pass unnoticed in a crowd," because " the
whole modern tendency of realistic fiction
is against oddness in a prominent figure."

So *The Old Wives' Tale* was inspired. It
fulfilled its inspiration. But at the risk of
seeming irrelevant, I must add other details.
Arnold Bennett had already, in 1903,
planned a novel about a woman of forty
(*Leonora*). He had long regarded Guy de
Maupassant's *Une Vie* as a supreme novel,
but he meant to go beyond *Une Vie*, or at
any rate to go as far. *The Old Wives' Tale*
was a deliberately vast undertaking. In
fact, it was too vast for accomplishment at
first. " For several years I looked my pro-
ject squarely in the face at intervals, and
then walked away to write novels of smaller

scope, of which I produced five or six."
The book was eventually begun in 1907, and
finished, after an interval, in 1908. It was
not all the cold-blooded, joyless thing it was
meant to be. Sophia, the beautiful sister,
was added. " Constance was the original
[heroine] ; Sophia was created out of
bravado, just to indicate that I declined
to consider Guy de Maupassant as the last
forerunner of the deluge."

There is the anatomy of authorship. The
book began in a great idea. It carried out
the idea after a long time, and with an addition. In the meanwhile, the Five Towns
democrat wrote for a living, just as nine
authors out of ten cannot fail to write. I
have just criticised those " novels of smaller
scope." Consider now what the larger scope
of the Five Towns novels means.

And, first of all, observe that Arnold
Bennett explicitly acknowledges the influence of de Maupassant. He says that " in
the nineties we used to regard *Une Vie* with
mute awe " : he identifies the formative

epoch thus clearly. He ranges himself with those who, like him, first attained fame, or at any rate attention, in *The Yellow Book*. Now the epoch immediately preceding Arnold Bennett's apprenticeship to literature, though it abbreviated the circumstances, liked to point its moral just as neatly and plainly as did the epoch of Dickens and Thackeray.[1] Novels were outwardly sleek and rounded, like a pigling of Epicurus' herd. The age of Yellerbocky, on the other hand, was learning its craft mainly from France, and despised both Victorian happinesses and late-Victorian mechanical skill. It went to another extreme, and left the rounding-off at the end to the sympathetic imagination of the reader—not seldom before he had contrived to understand the beginning. From the two strains of art (both, of course, still persisting), but chiefly

[1] " Life is monstrous, infinite, illogical, abrupt and poignant; a work of art, in comparison, is neat, finite, self-contained, rational, flowing, and emasculate."— R. L. STEVENSON, *Memories and Portraits*.

from the French, sprang a third, of which many novelists of to-day—Joseph Conrad, Arnold Bennett, sometimes H. G. Wells, and most of the younger writers—are practitioners. It is French, with a difference —French in artistic conception, English in thorough and laborious execution. In its products a central idea or a central tract of life focuses great masses of detail.

English fiction, in fact, since, roughly speaking, 1900, has shown a new breadth and courage. Often, it is true, a promising writer reveals that he has not sufficient spaciousness or steadiness of experience to live up to his ambitions. But the spirit of a fresh impulse is there. It might be urged, not without a great deal of truth, that the impulse is but a vital quickening of old ashes partially quenched —a return to the largeness of Dickens and Thackeray, and of Fielding and Richardson still farther back. Certainly to-day's novels have the same long vision and free range of treatment. But the great

novels of the eighteenth and nineteenth
centuries [1] were class novels, written from
a class point of view. Dickens, for all his
liberalism, could neither draw a gentleman
nor refrain from trying to do so. Thackeray,
for all his profound humanity, could draw
nothing but men and women bound hand
and foot by caste—gentlemen or their in-
feriors. In the new school there is neither
high nor low. Nor is there a necessary beginning or end, except the beginning of birth
and the end of death. The characteristic
achievement is controlled mass. A modern
novel is like a modern battle. A thousand
circumstances vibrate and vanish, sometimes with little apparent inter-connection.
So vivid and real are the details that often
they, and not the whole movement, linger
in the memory. Even at the " end "
the result may be vague. But the reader
and the novelist have taken part in a battle

[1] I do not mean exactly 1700-1900; the period
ends about 1870, when Meredith and Hardy were
beginning to attract notice.

of the soul. They have seen life together, and the reader, willy-nilly, has had to face what the author decrees to be reality. There is no ease here; letters are no longer the adornment of a graceful existence, nor fiction the recreation of a mind unbent. There is also no judgment upon life by the voice of old and honourable tradition; novelists are no longer the highest and most generous product of a classical education, nor the vigorous progeny of a sentimental nationalism. They are men—the biological summit of the ages. Science, in fact, has invaded fiction by colouring, imperceptibly but indelibly, the minds of those who reflect at all. Novels to-day are a chemical analysis of life, which is a compound of emotions, impressions and volitions.

How far, then, do the Five Towns novels achieve the ideal of *Une Vie* ? How far are they "realistic fiction" of the modern type ? Let us follow Aristotle's method, and take first the mean or perfect example, and afterwards the defects and the excesses.

74

The Old Wives' Tale appears, to a cursory glance, a formless chronicle; it is in reality a miracle of constructive genius and eclectic self-restraint. It is easily described as the lives of two women born in Bursley just before 1850, daughters of the great draper of St Luke's Square. One married her father's manager and continued to possess and control the shop, until she retired in favour of her chief assistant. The other, Sophia, married a flashy scoundrel, who deserted her in Paris a little before the siege; she, too, came back to Bursley to die. And that is the whole story, in a sense. It is the whole story of many lives; youth, marriage, the inexorable swift passage of the devouring years, adhesion to a place, death. Arnold Bennett tells it in such a manner that he never comments upon the two old wives; he never criticises the society in which they live; he never dwells upon any figure or thing in such a way that it stands out disproportionately from its environment; his own opinions, his sequence of ideas, his arrangement of the successive incidents, are wholly concealed. The book is just a chronicle, told with such profound art, such equableness and perfection of construction, that it might be written by some spirit in another world a thousand years hence.

A man who can thus set down the pages of change that make up the continuous book of existence, who can withhold himself from a philosophy of what he tells so austerely, who can excite pity with the use of never a pitiful word, is a great novelist. There is no English novel quite like *The Old Wives' Tale*. Its apparently endless succession of small prosaic things is a sustained effort of imagination all the more remarkable because there is no imagination visible in the plain tale. The book reflects all the breadth and the narrowness, all the strength and impotence, of the English middle class; of England, perhaps. In spite of our sentiment—the sentimentality despised by Bernard Shaw—there is a curious foundation of steady hard pessimism in the English character, and a still steadier endurance; both hopelessly inarticulate. Our flippant optimism of speech, and our reluctance to face any moral question fairly and squarely, are the mask of a grim distrust of life. "He had once been young, and he had grown old, and was now dead. That was all. Everything came to that."

In only one other novel has Arnold Bennett reached the same height of passionless austerity. Even *Clayhanger* and its companion, *Hilda Lessways*—two out of a promised three instalments of the life of a young, sensitive, timid Five Townsman and the highly-strung girl whom he is eventually to marry—even these two books are not quite on the same plane as *The Old Wives' Tale*, fine though they are. *Clayhanger*, indeed, is written from the outside. But it is written by one plainly tolerant and amused, not dispassionate and far away. It has the defect of personal intrusion by the author. *Hilda Lessways* is much more objective.

It may be interpolated here, as a piece

of literary intelligence, that *Clayhanger* and *Hilda Lessways*—the one, so to speak, a concurrent sequel to the other—are not coterminous, nor anything like it.

Edwin and Hilda had to wait long (as " Max " amusingly pointed out) before they went on with their journey. The third volume of the trilogy, *These Twain*, did not appear till five years after *Hilda Lessways*; and while it rounds off the story, it is the least striking of the three.

But after a period during which it seemed as if the author could never get back to his highest standard, he suddenly did so with *Riceyman Steps* (1923) — a masterly and even profound study of half-a-dozen people living in Clerkenwell, and especially of two misers. It is not a Five Towns novel, but is mentioned here because it alone can stand beside *The Old Wives' Tale*.

The isolation of the author's personality from his subject is seen equally in *Anna of the Five Towns*, a work often underrated, and of very high value. Its weaknesses are a certain lack of control over the digressions (an imperfect welding—it was the author's first novel of large " scope ") and what would in a lesser book be a virtue—a dramatic plot, which shows a tendency to let action dominate psychology too conveniently. I will not survey the book in detail. It is a study of three characters, virtually.[1] In the conclusion, in particular, the abstinence from compassion and the utter simplicity of language excite pity more forcibly than any emphasis could. *Leonora*—the story of a woman of charm and fine character married to a specious rogue—is a work of distinction on much the same level as *Anna of the Five Towns*, and subject to the same criticism. *Whom God hath Joined* has the defects of both the modern and the Victorian novel. It looks at first sight like a polemical tract on divorce and its anomalies; but as a matter of fact it presents two well-balanced but not wholly typical divorce cases, and the real issue is the effect of the Divorce Court, with its odious publicity, on the persons con-

[1] Dramatised as *Cupid and Commonsense*. See p. 100.

cerned, more especially on a pure young girl. It is neither entirely dramatic (not a *story*, that is), nor entirely realistic. It suffers from a certain unevenness of execution and irresolution of aim, though it contains some remarkable passages.

The Price of Love, from a technical point of view, is admirably constructed, but not dispassionate enough. In scope, it is almost an artistic relapse. It is a particular, not a universal, book. It is a minute study of five people, and chiefly of one of the five, a girl of the lower middle class who married a rogue and only gradually discovered that he was a rogue. On every page the author is clearly enthusiastic; he is intensely interested in every shade of feeling, every reaction to stimulus, every logical foundation of emotions obscure and dumb. He has never shown a surer mastery than in the picture of Rachel's attitude to Mrs Maldon and the abominable Batchgrew, of her quarrel with Louis, of Louis's brief glimpse deep into his own mean soul when he is found out.

But the author's attitude in the book is not objective. He is not recording life, but some lives; the only vision he gives is of a particular instance of the eternal loyalty of woman. His power of observation is as true as ever, and even more acutely comprehensive; the nature of his subject itself tends to narrow his philosophy for the time.

I can say nothing in detail of the three volumes of short stories (*Tales of the Five Towns, The Grim Smile of the Five Towns,* and *The Matador of the Five Towns*). They support every criticism, favourable or unfavourable. Their variety is very striking. They range from mere tabloid melodramas to little transcripts from life, from neat, smooth comedies to unspoilt tragedy. They suffer more than the novels from Arnold Bennett's want of verbal imagination : they gain more than the novels from his indifference to bright colours and his economy of words.

So far, then, Arnold Bennett is seen to have tried, and tried more successfully than

F　81

not, to set down his vision of life without explicitly adding his views of it—to chronicle soberly, seriously, things as they are, allowing local conditions to create their own atmosphere; for, prosaic, detailed, photographic as they may seem, the Five Towns novels are full of atmosphere. It is curious to notice the nearly parallel experience, and the utterly different craftsmanship, of H. G. Wells. He too knew drapers' shops and the middle class; he took advice from Mr Lewis Hind; he even describes the Five Towns, in *The New Machiavelli*; but except for some little ornamental accidents, he writes as an Englishman, as a set-scene novelist working from a beginning through a middle to an end, and as an outside critic of an existing order rather than its mouthpiece. He is not an egotist in the Five Towns sense.

There remain, however, three Five Towns novels uncriticised, and a passage from the already quoted preface not illustrated. Arnold Bennett inserted Sophia in *The Old Wives' Tale* " out of bravado." He wrote,

one cannot help thinking, these three novels
—*Helen with the High Hand* (dramatised in
1914), *The Card*, and *The Regent*—from the
same motive : they are at least *bravura.*

Two of them need not be discussed at any
length. *Helen with the High Hand* (1910)
tells how a formidable young woman made
her formidable uncle go into Five Towns
society and buy a large house, and how both
she and the uncle were married eventually
to suitable persons. It is a jocular perform-
ance, amusing when one can forget the in-
trinsic vulgarity of nature and manners of
the characters; the author seems to regard
them as charming to other people as well as
to their own circle. That is one of Arnold
Bennett's inherent weaknesses—that he
often assumes, or appears to assume, that
the world at large would regard the society
of the Five Towns as that society regards
itself. *The Regent* (1913) is a sequel to *The
Card*, and is an account of how its hero, by
impudence, shrewdness, luck and sometimes
something very like dishonesty, indulged

in a theatrical venture and conquered London as he had already conquered the Five Towns. It is full of diversion; but it suffers seriously from the fact that the London characters are hopelessly superficial and unrealised, in contrast to the living and breathing Five Townspeople. Both novels are essentially Victorian in treatment— fantasias, in effect, but locally realistic.

The Card is also really a fantasia. But it is something else as well. It is what painters used to call " The Portrait of a Gentleman " —a picture, that is, of someone whom they regarded as at least admirable. *The Card* is a very disturbing book. The man who could write it is a complete master of technique. It is episodic, but perfectly constructed, and the manner of it exquisitely suited to the humour of the conception. Ironic commercialism, the crafty triumphs of an alert, yet unconscious, financial genius, have never been so vivaciously and faithfully rendered. Nor is an occasional gentleness lacking. The disturbing features are two—that the Card himself is presented as the pride and fine flower of Five Towns life, and that Arnold Bennett also must be strongly suspected of admiring him. Now Denry Machin, a successful Five Towns financier, was something very like a robber. He began by falsifying his marks at school; and the author justifies it by saying that Denry was "not uncommonly vicious. Every schoolboy is dishonest, by the adult standard." He proceeded to tamper with his employer's papers, to act as an unregistered moneylender (at five hundred and twenty per cent. per annum—threepence a week on each half-crown), to break off an engagement by deliberate and cheap rudeness, and to bribe a footman to cause an opportune carriage accident. In fact, he possessed the business instinct in the highest degree, and his impulsiveness was sharpened to the finest point of slyness.

It would be foolish to insist that the chief character in a book must be conventionally good or moral, and, except when the thing becomes a dangerous cult, as it does sometimes in novels of crime, there is no reason on earth why roguery should not be treated either realistically or amusingly. Denry Machin is a very amusing person indeed, and by normal standards of dishonesty only mildly dishonest; the Llandudno scenes in particular are a joy. The trouble is that neither the novelist nor what he represents as Five Towns opinion even suspects the Card of falling below the average English level of honesty.

Except Edwin Clayhanger, Denry Machin is one of the author's most completely and carefully studied male characters; and he is, on a census of the persons in these novels, a more typical Five Townsman than Clayhanger. Here is a table of some important young Five Townsmen created by Arnold Bennett. It is a startling document. Of course, a "hero" need not be heroic. But this census almost suggests that honesty is the worst policy, to be followed only by timid or repellent dullards.

ARNOLD BENNETT

NOVEL	PERSON	CHARACTER	POSITION
Clayhanger	Edwin Clayhanger	Timid, thoughtful	Printer
"	Willie Orgreaves	Decent, lively	Doctor
Hilda Lessways	George Cannon	Bigamous, dishonest	Speculator
Whom God hath Joined	Lawrence Ridware	Decent, timid	Solicitor
"	Mark Ridware	Decent, lively, artistic	Artist
	George Fearns	Liar, adulterous	Solicitor
The Price of Love	Louis Fores	Liar, thief	Pottery-maker
"	Julian Maldon	Thief, puritan, uncouth	"
The Old Wives' Tale	Gerald Scales	Dishonest, adulterous	Commercial traveller
"	Samuel Povey	Honest, plodding	Draper
"	Cyril Povey	Slack, shifty, specious	Artist
	Dick Povey	Honest, alert	Motor-maker
The Card	Edward Henry Machin	Sharp, humorous, untruthful	Financier, commission agent
Anna of the Five Towns	Henry Mynors	Pushing, hearty, rather hard	Pottery-maker
"	Willie Price	Timid, oppressed, forger	"
Leonora	John Stanway	Dishonest, able, flashy	"
Helen with the High Hand	Andrew Dean	Honest, rather uncouth	"
"	Emanuel Prockter	Showy, snobbish, apparently foolish	"

There are many similar portraits in the short stories, but they would not affect appreciably any generalisation based upon the above list. There are also many minor young gentleman, the Swetnams, the Etches, the Clayton Vernons, and others, of whom we are told little more than that they delight in fine raiment and the ostentation of

87

wealth; a disposition not peculiar to the Five Towns.

Consider also—in order to gauge how far realism and bravado clash in these works—the general society described in them. The Five Towns young man, in addition to showing the qualities already tabulated, is cheaply and inadequately educated. He is first and foremost practical, which means, as a rule, that he hates long views, scientific technical knowledge, and careful organisation. He is for a considerable time in utter subservience to the older generation. His chief aim in life is to get money; to dress and behave smartly; to marry, but not always to be pedantically monogamous. He has few standards of conduct; he is sharp, and his sharpness is of the kind which breaks the spirit, not the letter, of the law. He has no sanction of restraint except the fear of consequences. He visits Llandudno or Man in August and behaves in the manner of a specious " nut "; sometimes he attains Brighton; nowhere else in England is he at home. He drinks to a comfortable extent, goes to Association football matches, and is generally of a brisk and knowing demeanour. He knows life; but it is difficult not to feel that his knowledge, like that of the young gentleman detained in Mr Namby's office, has been gained " through the dirty panes of glass in a bar door."

Growing older, prospering, and wriggling out of the constriction of the paternal rule, he begins to drive a dog-cart. He becomes a member of a club; and perhaps there is no more ignoble place on earth than the professional and trade club of a provincial town. Æsthetic tastes develop slightly; in particular, he is genuinely and profoundly musical, and, with an abundance of boorish directness, plays duets of classical music. He may collect books; pictures, never. He may even learn something of the history, traditions, and aspirations of the potter's craft. On the other hand, he may juggle insecurely with finance, and tamper with the purity of his home. In fact, when Arnold

Bennett writes of " the average sensual man," he means, if his " heroes " are any criterion, " the sensual average man." Of course he happens to be able to draw nasty men with peculiar skill and fulness, so that the evil they do lives disproportionately in the memory. But there are only six Five Townsmen in the census whom he has invested at once with virtue and a certain charm : Edwin Clayhanger and his friend " the Sunday," Mr Orgreaves, Dick Povey, Mark Ridware and Willie Price (a forger, it is true, but with the strongest extenuating circumstances). Denry Machin is virtuous, but not charming. All the rest are low, or mean, or flashy, or hard, or stuffy ; but they are not all criminal. They are merely business men ; bearded, rather hot, piggy-eyed, pushing, often horribly efficient, or else rather cringing, or rather sharp, or unconsciously hypocritical.

That is to-day's generation. Their fathers were singularly prone to become widowers early in life, and afterwards to develop all the least desirable traits of puritanism : utter, relentless strictness, domestic tyranny, oppression of rivals, vile manners, hatred of ideas and ideals. Fortunately, they usually had a stroke in late middle age, and became harrowingly helpless. At such an opportunity, the chief son or daughter seized and used the fallen sceptre.

These old men of Arnold Bennett's, indeed, are a nightmare. Darius Clayhanger, Eli Boothroyd, Ephraim Tellwright, Batchgrew, John Baines, Critchlow, Eli Machin, old Brunt—there is not one who is not ignorant and cruel, domineering and boorish, physically nauseating and socially non-existent. And yet they are powerful figures, not unworthy of respect ; hard men facing a hard world proudly.

The female differs, and is on the whole more pleasing. She seems to fulfil one or other of two implied natural laws—that woman is the plaything, the adored plaything of man, often broken, or that she is the huntress, generally successful but always pursuing, with the arts of allurement and victorious concession highly developed.

The men in Arnold Bennett's books enjoy themselves in their way; I cannot recall one of his women who is really happy, except perhaps the delightfully drawn Mrs Sutton in *Anna of the Five Towns*. Their nearest approach to joy is humourless acceptance of comfort. The middle class is still predominantly Victorian in the habits of life; and the women have to be domestic, whether aggressively or receptively, whether hunter or hunted. They have, like the men, their own freemasonry. The men know their own vices, and never give one another away. The women never give away to the men their universal tolerant perception of male weakness.

Such is the society of that remarkable district of England, and so do the egotism and mentality of Arnold Bennett unite to picture it. He rises above his subject in the better part of all these novels, and entirely in *The Old Wives' Tale*; he identifies himself with it, takes its aggressive, defiant point of view, sinks with it, in other parts, chiefly when he achieves humour. Now recall again *The Card*. It, or rather its hero, has one quality I have not dwelt upon yet. Denry's chief characteristic is what Hobbes calls laughter: " Sudden glory, the passion which is caused by some sudden act of their own that pleaseth them "; and glory is an " exultation of the mind, arising from imagination of a man's own power and ability." An irresistible splendour and inspiration carry Denry on, while at the same time he is able to perceive his " own power and ability." The quality is not exactly vanity, nor is it exactly the conscious use of strength; it is midway between—a sort of overmastering, clear-headed humour. It is a quality displayed (I write in a purely Pickwickian sense) by Arnold Bennett himself. It is an inherent Quinturban gift. He is liable at any moment to seize an inspiration and (mentally) glory in it, feeling his power and indulging it with a freakish wilfulness; a most human frailty. Thackeray, I think, is said to have exclaimed upon his own success in writing a certain passage; Fielding, I am sure, must have felt sudden glory at moments in *Jonathan Wild*; Sterne is a perpetual Card. Arnold Bennett has given the Five Towns term to a larger world, and must himself be named by it.

The union of impersonal strength and personal bravado in Arnold Bennett, in fact, is his most characteristic trait. It makes it, however, very difficult to assess his outlook upon life justly. If we had not *The Old Wives' Tale*, and certain passages in *Clayhanger*, and the conclusions of *Anna of the Five Towns* and *The Price of Love*, the verdict would be hopelessly unfair. It would convict Arnold Bennett of knowingly accepting the egotistical, self-assertive, unlovely ideals of a community wholly commercial in thought and deed. In fact, one side of that community's existence is so far obscured by its commercial activity that

Arnold Bennett fails to give it reality. He takes no account of what is still a powerful thing in middle-class life—religion in one form or another. Wesleyanism is the Five Towns form. Arnold Bennett never understands it; it is as alien to his temperament—or at any rate to his artistic temperament—as love of natural beauty. He can describe vividly the frenzy of a revival; he does so in *Anna of the Five Towns,* with minuteness and outward accuracy. But compare such passages with the description in Harold Frederic's *Illumination,*[1] or the spirit of them with the spirit of "Mark Rutherford"; the Five Towns scenes have no life, no feeling for the underlying reality and torment of soul. However superficial a religion may be, it is the framework of some sort of philosophy of existence in those who hold to it. It is a defect of sympathy in Arnold Bennett that he does not appreciate that philosophy; or if he does, does not deal

[1] Published in America as *The Damnation of Theron Ware.*

with it in a series of novels which covers
almost every other aspect of the middle
class.

But the ignoble half of life, happily, is
not Arnold Bennett's chief or sole pre-
occupation. He has become, by taking
thought, a great novelist in regard to
technique. He can, moreover, see life
steadily and whole, as all great novelists
must; even though he turns Card now and
then and plays with it. He has also an
individual gift which sets him apart from
other novelists—his extraordinary power of
analysis. Henry James is the supreme
living possessor of such a power. He has
paid a high tribute to Arnold Bennett.
But his own power is differently applied;
it is intellectual rather than concrete.
Very seldom does Arnold Bennett show his
characters as searching their own souls. He
shows what is much more profoundly true
than any amount of introspection—that the
middle class are incapable of searching their
own souls; that Five Townsmen (like most

Englishmen) act upon a balance of considerations, but seldom think the considerations out; that impulse and inhibition are for ever struggling on the surface.

It is, then, as a Five Townsman, and upon the material of the Five Towns middle class, that Arnold Bennett works most happily. But just because he has genius he rises far above local conditions; and just because he is a Five Townsman he enjoys himself thoroughly—not least when he is privately laughing at those who would like him to do otherwise—in flouting the social and even the literary standards of persons born and bred in less favoured regions. But he cannot get into the minds of those persons if they are above the middle class. His "London" or cosmopolitan "high society" novels are often no more than Hall Caine or Corelli devoid of sloppiness. Directly he comes to a lower stratum, as in *Riceyman Steps*, he once more sees life steadily and whole.

VI

STAGE PLAYS

NOT all Arnold Bennett's plays have been successfully produced. The earliest were *Cupid and Common-sense* (produced in 1908), *What the Public Wants* (1909), *The Great Adventure* (1911 ; not produced in London till 1913) ; *The Honeymoon* (1911) ; and (in collaboration) *Milestones*. His three *Polite Farces for the Drawing-Room* were published as a book in 1899.

"My aim in writing plays," he affirmed in 1900, "whether alone or in collaboration, has always been strictly commercial. I wanted money in heaps, and I wanted advertisement for my books." It is only to be expected, in such circumstances, that the *Polite Farces* should not be works of genius. Nor are they worthy of con-sideration as works of art. There are three of them, and they are all three purely mechanical. Emotions change in them with the rapidity and slickness peculiar to farce, where a door has but to slam to alter any train of causation. The dialogue has the stilted gentlemanliness also peculiar to farce of the drawing-room type; the English middle class has always been prone to think periphrasis the highest form of wit. The *Polite Farces*, in fact, are in no way representative of " the intelligent imaginative writer" whom, in the preface to his first-produced play, Arnold Bennett demands for the modern English theatre. They are not intelligent and they are not imaginative. They are effective in an entirely conventional way.

Their belated successor, *Cupid and Commonsense*, was produced by the Stage Society. It is a dramatic version of *Anna of the Five Towns*, with, however, a very different ending. The names are all altered from those in the novel, but the events and even some of the dialogue are the same up

to the end of the third act. The fourth
act is very instructive. Eli Boothroyd
(Ephraim Tellwright of the novel) has
forced his daughter Alice (Anna) to oppress
Willie Beach (Willie Price) and his father,
who owed her money. Beach *père*, like
Price *père*, committed suicide; Willie went
to America. There the third act ends, at
the point where the novel ends. The predominant crisis of the play (thitherto) and
the book—the ultimate rebellion of the
repressed, timid girl against her hard,
tyrannical father—has been fully developed.
Willie has been shown as a weak, helpless,
honest, pathetic boy, of whom it would not
be unreasonable to expect the sudden tragic
despair and resolution which ends his life
in the novel. But in Act IV. of the play he
comes back to England happy and prosperous, with an American wife (they are
faintly like Sam and his wife in *Milestones*)
—" no longer miserable, and so objection-
able." Eli Boothroyd meanwhile has had
a stroke (that favourite Five Towns catas-

trophe, and is a pitiable, impotent doll.
The focus, therefore, has shifted from the
domestic struggle to the psychology of
Willie and Alice, who, together or separately,
are all the main interest left.

The effect of this is that Willie and Alice,
in Acts I.-III., under Boothroyd's dominion,
seem to be mere sheep; reluctant sheep,
but still sheep. But in Act IV. they have
become, so to speak, well-fed pug-dogs.
The transmutation has taken place entirely
" off." In Acts I.-III. they are timid; in
Act IV., smug. All the stages of transition
are omitted, and they are presented as
utterly different people. The play cannot
therefore be realised as a continuous picture
of developing life.

A hostile critic might suspect the fourth
act of being a device for avoiding the tragic
ending. It is more sympathetic to say that
drama has the drawbacks of life. In life
very few persons follow acutely all the
minute emotions of their friends and foes,
and actions are far more visible and signifi-

cant than thoughts—of course, in daily traffic only, not in results or influence. A deed, like personality itself, is a direct and immediate stimulus to another person; but only a very nimble mind can follow certainly and immediately the processes of thought which are behind the spoken word. The act of reading allows time for understanding those processes, and the provision of fuller corroborative detail. The act of sight is too swift for most people; an audience of Henry Jameses or Arnold Bennetts or James Barries is impossible. Plays must, therefore, be written for slightly less vivacious persons. This play fails in that respect.

I do not mean by this that " the intelligent, imaginative writer " is not to write for the stage, or that he will never find an intelligent, imaginative audience. It is simply a question of degree or (physiologically) of the speed of reaction to stimulus. Some few people react very readily to very slight stimuli; we call them " quick " or " sympathetic." Many hardly react at all unless the stimulus is blunt and heavy; hence the popularity of musical comedy and comedians with protuberant waists. To borrow an illustration from a kindred branch of stage art. Mephistopheles in red looks very tremendous against a black background. But you, the "producer," want to make him look even more coldly diabolical, and you think a little green light would have the desired result. You get the green to a certain density, very hopefully—and then Mephistopheles simply vanishes; literally, he becomes invisible to anyone a few yards away. The green and red rays have played with the optic nerve, and Mephistopheles cannot be seen. It is a trick of optics. So the failure to get a good deal of psychology from speaker to hearer is a trick of mental optics; æsthetics, to give the thing the proper name. The right mixture of rays is not in the last act of *Cupid and Common-sense*.

I have dwelt on this point more fully than is really warranted by the discussion of a

single play. It is necessary, because that
play, when published, contained a well-
reasoned polemical preface denouncing the
unintelligence of most English theatres, and
demanding intelligent dramas by intelligent
dramatists. Arnold Bennett says that
there are plenty of such plays to be had.
The accusation and the statement are both
entirely true. But there is a great deal more
in the dramatic stimulus than an appeal to
the intelligence. The preface to *Cupid and
Commonsense* implies that there is not; the
play itself proved that there is. It is, of all
Arnold Bennett's performed plays, the one
which contains the most profound single or
main idea—that of the conflict between
sense and commonsense, feeling and reason.
All his plays *are*, as a matter of fact, plays
with main ideas, even that delightful
fantasia, *The Great Adventure*. *Cupid and
Commonsense* goes deeper than any. Its
failure comes from the fact that its depth is
uneven, shifting, and not to be charted—at
one moment " dramatic," at another mental.

However, the play certainly vindicated its author's claim to intelligence and imagination. It was followed, in 1909, by a comedy in which intelligence lit up a certain large and disturbing phenomenon of modern English life. *What the Public Wants* is the dramatic expression of the spirit underlying *The Truth about an Author* ; and it is just as faithful and terrible a piece of realism. But the public did not know it. The expert is seldom tremendous enough to be a prophet as well, and the audience he deserves treats him either as a Blue book, too heavy to digest, or as a reed shaken by the wind. *What the Public Wants* could be popular only when it describes what the public no longer wants ; when it had ripened, in fact, into a comedy of manners. It is still a play for the small theatre and the select audience ; and in such a setting it was fully appreciated in 1923.

It deals, like Mr Montague's *Hind Let Loose*, with the mixture of self-deception and conscious deception of the public which inspires a newspaper. It is a faithful portrait of a great newspaper proprietor, who states his creed quite frankly:

"I've no desire at all to ram my personal ideas down the throats of forty different publics. I give each what it wants. I'm not a blooming reformer. I'm a merchant."

(The final sentence provokes the grimly true retort, "On Sundays you're a muck merchant.") Such are the views of Sir Charles Worgan, Arnold Bennett's Napoleon of the press. They are the views which, it cannot be denied, are behind certain manifestations of the English newspaper. And there are only two answers to them. One is the policeman. But no judge and no jury would convict such a prisoner as Worgan. The other answer is indicated by Arnold Bennett. There will come at long last a rainy day for the unmoral, capricious, press without ideals, when "the public will want something better than you can give it." Education, that efficiency of soul as of conduct which Arnold Bennett is for ever ingeminating, will be the death of the " office-boy press."

There is no other version of *What the Public Wants*; it affords no contrast between literature and speech as means of expression. In *The Great Adventure* we return to that contrast. The play is a dramatic version of that excellent " tale of these days," *Buried Alive*. I do not know which was written first, nor does it matter, though it would be an interesting revelation; the book was first published in 1908, the play first acted in 1911. The play had a prodigious run. As everybody knows, it deals with a great painter (" the only question which cultured persons felt it their duty to believe was whether he was the greatest painter who ever lived or merely the greatest painter since Velasquez ") who, out of shyness, let his valet be buried in Westminster Abbey in mistake for himself, and was eventually discovered to be alive.

The idea of a great man has always had a

lure for Arnold Bennett. In this book and this play he realises it more fully than elsewhere; in the play especially. He solves an author's most difficult problem—the problem of persuading his audience of his meaning without explaining it in so many words. He had to give, and he gave, through Mr Ainley, by Mr Ainley's help in giving suitable expression to the words provided, an impression of intellectual eminence—a feeling that the painter was capable of the great achievements attributed to him, and was not a mere piece in a mosaic.

A few weeks after the appearance of *The Great Adventure* in Glasgow, *The Honeymoon* was presented at the Royalty Theatre, London. It had the advantage of an almost perfect cast. But that advantage was, in a sense, a defect, because *The Honeymoon* is exactly what the law labels it—a stage play, and Miss Marie Tempest and Mr Graham Browne did not have to work to turn it into real life. It is amusing. A writer of so strong an ironic humour as

Arnold Bennett must necessarily make some fun out of his central situation— the refusal of a bride to shorten her honeymoon in order to let her aviator husband fly over Snowdon before a German rival can do so, and the very opportune discovery that their marriage (just celebrated) was void because the officiating curate was a sham. The discussion, however (it is not unduly complicated by action), lasts through three acts. The dialogue is often banal, and the secondary characters are all lay-figures, grouped, not living and moving individuals. The play as a whole is too close to that school of drama which has made the adjective "dramatic" synonymous with "unreal" or "improbable." It is the work of a man obviously capable of modernity, but reverting to the type-comedy of Byron and Robertson. One would like to learn that it was one of those plays written early, but held up, as Arnold Bennett complains, by managers.

The most successful of the published or

produced plays of the author, *Milestones*, was produced on 5th March 1912. It is, however, not entirely by Arnold Bennett, and should properly not be considered in this book, unless one were exactly aware of the extent of his collaboration. It would be dangerous to dogmatise about it. I am told that when Mr Comyns Carr and Mr Stephen Phillips collaborated in a grievous version of *Faust*, all the highly skilled literary critics fell a-choosing the parts each author ought to have written, or to be ashamed of having written; with the result that the poetic achievement of Mr Carr was very gratifyingly ascribed to Mr Phillips. So I do not propose to try to dissever Mr Knoblauch, part-author of *Milestones*, from Mr Bennett. I only wish here to quote the closing words, words used a hundred times during life by every Englishman. The granddaughter, radiant, triumphant in youth and beauty and the knowledge of to-day, has gone out tenderly, leaving Sir John Rhead and his wife alone—old

lovers, with all the asperities of a life's
intercourse dimmed and forgotten. That
pretty Victorian tinkle of *Juanita* sounds
from the next room, sung by the old maid
who has solved, in her barren disappoint-
ment, all the mystery of human sorrow :

JOHN (*looking at the flower*).   We live and
learn.

ROSE (*nodding her head*).   Yes, John.

I neither know nor care which author contrived that gentle " curtain."   But it might
have been written at the end of each of
Arnold Bennett's greatest books.

The later plays have not had the same long
run as *Milestones* and *The Great Adventure*.
Judith—dramatised from the Apocrypha—is
a strange mixture of colloquialisms, Wardour
Street English, journalese, and Dickens :
they do not go well with the Old Testament
spirit of the grim story.   *The Title* deserved
a longer run ; the fatigue that accompanies
incessant judgment perhaps affected the
rather hostile critics.   It is as good a social
satire as *What the Public Wants*.   *The Love*

Match (1922) depends almost entirely upon dialogue and two surprises, rather "in the air." I have not had an opportunity of seeing *Body and Soul* (1922) acted, but it is very amusing reading. The distribution of plot and talk is uneven.

Arnold Bennett is competent and skilled as a dramatist, but does not climb the steep ascent of imaginative triumph. If he could put upon the stage, with kindred reticence and sincerity, such a scene as the farewell between Anna and Willie Price, or as Sophia Scales's last sight of her husband in the upper room at Manchester, or such a piece of atmosphere as is breathed in Clayhanger's first visit to the Orgreaves, then he would give to the drama "timber, or a piece of the world discovered." [1]

---

[1] The "privately printed" *Don Juan de Marana* (1923) was produced at a price which forbade me to read it. From a public review of this esoteric work I borrow a quotation from the playwright: "The fatal mischief with the modern play is inadequacy, insignificance, puerility, absurdity of theme. . . . The theme is the most important thing."

VII

TO-DAY AND TO-MORROW

IT may seem, perhaps, that too many of the foregoing pages have been devoted to pointing out blemishes in the Five Towns and weaknesses in the novelist produced by them. I have been dealing with two things, with Arnold Bennett and with a state of society. Neither is quite like anything else in English literature, and if I have emphasised failure rather than success it is because the partial failure of a new product is more instructive than its complete and easy success. Let me explain now why and how Arnold Bennett and his work are new.

I have said that the society he describes, and I have implied that his point of view in describing it, is middle class: purely and really of the very middle, in mind, body and estate. I have pointed out local conditions which in-bred that society and isolated it from the general current of world-culture, except in regard to music and a few refinements of material comfort. And I have suggested that it belongs to a marked epoch of industrial evolution. Now neither that epoch nor that society has ever appeared in English fiction before ; nor has any novelist of middle or higher industrial life ever presented his material with such a literary equipment and outlook as Arnold Bennett possesses. That is the great and new importance of his work.

It is a suggestive fact that a commercial nation like England should lack great novels of commerce. There are plenty of romances of business, plenty of fictitious indictments of business methods, plenty of stories of the squalor and contrasts of a commercially organised society. There are a few great novels of industrial life : Mrs Gaskell's, for instance. But no one hitherto, so far as I know, has not merely portrayed the life of the middle class manu-

facturer but spoken with his voice. When
H. G. Wells is dealing with trade, he is
criticising it from the standpoint of intelligent socialism—deploring its want of education, admiring its bravery and pathos,
hating its mechanical, anti-social merciless-
ness. When William de Morgan describes
the lower middle class, he does so with a
reserve of his own idealism. When Upton
Sinclair, or James Bryce, or Oliver Onions,
or May Sinclair, or any similar novelist of
eminence touches the middle and lower
strata in one way or another, there is always
a different, alien ideal in their work. In the
Five Towns novels there is no ideal. There
is no criticism. There is no tradition or
philosophy of society. There is nothing but
life as the people described live it and see it
and feel it.

It may or may not be for the good of
England in general that such a life is lived
by such people. But it is very much for the
good of English literature that a writer can
so profoundly master his art as to present

this passionless panorama of life. I have spoken of Arnold Bennett's efficiency: it is a Five Towns virtue, appreciated and desired by Five Townsmen. But it must not be confused with this infinitely higher artistic efficiency—this selflessness, this steady, inexorable, faithful comprehension of mind and power of expression. That also is new in England, though it is not peculiar to Arnold Bennett. It is the new spirit of English fiction, working to maintain and to advance the glory of a form of art which in this country has had a history full of honour. The English novel will not suffer through such a spirit. It will rather grow to the measure of that vaster civilisation which we are only just beginning.

It is not in all his books, not even in a majority of them, that Arnold Bennett reaches this height. Perhaps only one writer living to-day has shown the power of being always at the same pitch of soul (I say nothing now of expression or subject): Thomas Hardy, with whom Arnold Bennett has much more in common than the utter external dissimilarity of their books suggests. If all his novels were on the same plane as *The Old Wives' Tale*, Arnold Bennett would have recreated English fiction (he has already, like H. G. Wells, had a great influence upon younger writers). What he will ultimately achieve I cannot hope to prophesy. It can at least be said of him with confidence that even in late middle life he seems able to surpass, in almost any direction, all except his very best work yet done. He is not like Galba and many modern novelists—*capax imperii, nisi imperasset* ; he has realised his own promise, and he still keeps the promise alive.

At the same time, he has the little weaknesses of his individual virtues. He is so efficient that he economises details, as I have pointed out. He is so skilled that he may not always realise the unevenness of labour easily accomplished. He has that occasional cocksureness of a Card, that inability to perceive local or provincial limitations. He has an unfortunate mediocrity of style in keeping with his own definition of that almost indefinable thing:

" Style cannot be distinguished from matter. When a writer conceives an idea he conceives it in a form of words. That form of words constitutes his style, and it is absolutely governed by the idea. The idea can only exist in words, and it can only exist in one form of words. You cannot say exactly the same thing in two different ways." (*Literary Taste*, chap. vi.)

There are debatable points in that formula, but it suffices. Arnold Bennett's style varies directly as his matter, except that he really does write bad English now and then, when the matter is not necessarily bad. In his matter there is no bright colour: he uses few images—he thinks in things, not in pictures. By education and training he relies upon a vocabulary that is unrelievedly plain: a primrose is a primrose to him—I am not sure that it is even yellow; and he employs words for what they denote, not for what they connote. The result is to make his victories more difficult, and (a curious irony) to necessitate the use of a great many severe grey words where another writer might have done as well with one purple one. There is no beauty in his English : yet there is beauty in some of the thoughts he suggests—thoughts which *will* exist, for every reader, in other words than those he uses. And, by another irony, he can paint.

The greyness, and the ugliness which it implies, I have ascribed to his environment. Almost one would think that men are born old in Bursley, so little sense of wonder and ecstasy do they show. There is but one hint of rapture (other than the cheerfulness of streets and crowds) in all the Five Towns novels—that recurrent mention of the garden of the Orgreaves in *Clayhanger*. Only once, as yet, has Arnold Bennett dealt with the first happiness of marriage—and then *The Price of Love* is disillusion. All his other characters are either but pupils being taught the grammar of life, or middle-aged and old people long weary of every syllable of it. Even Edwin Clayhanger had grown grave and preoccupied before he married Hilda; while Denry Machin has too strenuous a hold on the means of living to enjoy full life.

And yet there is the converse of that gravity to be weighed. When one has considered all the pettiness and coarseness and gloom of the Five Towns, there still remains something deeper, some quality not described, not mentioned, which makes Arnold Bennett's characters human. I should say that it is the spirit of freedom in them, the spirit for which their creator has so often argued so well. Much foolishness is talked in the name of liberty, much pomp has been given to a semblance of it with no atom of substance in it. But it is, in spite of all hypocrisies and servilities and cynicisms, the secret heritage which, all unconscious, Englishmen hand on one to another. These Five Townspeople live in it and by it. They

value their independence. They have one
and all a robust and confident bravery.
Yet they would laugh at the idea of uphold-
ing or proclaiming the Rights of Man. They
do not know that they themselves are the
embodiment of them. All their pride, their
bustling life, their concentrated, narrow
force, their ambitions and their courage, are
sprung from old freedom, and are the living
seeds of a growth into that wider, nobler
liberty towards which the army of man-
kind's night is for ever toiling.

A SHORT BIBLIOGRAPHY OF ARNOLD BENNETT'S PRINCIPAL WRITINGS

[Dates are given in square brackets preceded by N.D. when the book itself is not dated but can be dated accurately from other sources. New editions are only given when they involve material revision of text. The order is chronological.]

Journalism for Women. 1898.

A Man from the North (*Lane*). 1898. New edition (*Methuen*). 1912.

Polite Farces for the Drawing-Room (*Lumley*). 1899.

Sidney Yorke's Friend (*Wells Gardner*). N.D. [1901].

Fame and Fiction (*Grant Richards*). 1901.

Anna of the Five Towns: A Novel [see "Cupid and Commonsense"] (*Chatto & Windus*). 1902.

The Grand Babylon Hotel: A Fantasia on Modern Themes (*Chatto & Windus*). 1902.

The Gates of Wrath: A Melodrama (*Chatto & Windus*). 1903.

The Truth about an Author [Anonymous] (*Constable*). 1903. New edition [with author's name and new preface] (*Methuen*). 1914.

Leonora: A Novel (*Chatto & Windus*). 1903.

How to Become an Author: A Practical Guide (*Pearson*). 1903.

A Great Man: A Frolic (*Chatto & Windus*). 1904.

Teresa of Watling Street: A Fantasia on Modern Themes (*Chatto & Windus*). 1904.

Tales of the Five Towns (*Chatto & Windus*). 1905.
Sacred and Profane Love: A Novel in Three Episodes (*Chatto & Windus*). 1905. As a play, 1919 (*Chatto*).

The Loot of Cities: Being the Adventures of a Millionaire in Search of Joy: A Fantasia (*Alston Rivers*). 1904.

ARNOLD BENNETT

Hugo: A Fantasia on Modern Themes (*Chatto & Windus*) 1906.

Whom God Hath Joined (*Nutt*). 1906.

Things That Interested Me: Being Leaves from a Journal Kept by Arnold Bennett. With a preface by G. Sturt (*Privately Printed ; Burslem*). 1906. See below.

The Ghost: A Fantasia on Modern Times [*sic*] (*Chatto & Windus*). 1907.

The Grim Smile of the Five Towns (*Chapman & Hall*). 1907.

The City of Pleasure: A Fantasia on Modern Themes (*Chatto & Windus*). 1907.

The Reasonable Life: Being Hints for Men and Women [see " Mental Efficiency," below] (*Fifield*). 1907.

How to Live on Twenty-Four Hours a Day [? first published, 1907]. New edition, with new preface (*Hodder & Stoughton*). 1912.

Buried Alive: A Tale of These Days [see " The Great Adventure "] (*Chapman & Hall*). 1908.

What the Public Wants: A Play in Four Acts [first acted, 1909] (Special Supplement to " The English Review ") 1909. New edition [in book form] (*Palmer*). 1910.

The Old Wives' Tale: A Novel (*Chapman & Hall*). 1908. New edition, with new preface (*Hodder & Stoughton*). 1912.

The Human Machine (*New Age Press*). 1908.

Cupid and Commonsense: A Play in Four Acts [dramatic version of " Anna of the Five Towns " ; first acted, 1908] (*Palmer*). 1909.

The Glimpse: An Adventure of the Soul (*Chapman & Hall*). 1909.

Literary Taste: How to Form It (*New Age Press*). 1909.

Helen with the High Hand: An Idyllic Diversion (*Chapman & Hall*). 1910. Dramatic version, adapted by Richard Pryce (*Lacy*). 1914 ; produced in that year.

Clayhanger (*Methuen*). 1910.

The Honeymoon: A Comedy in Three Acts [first acted 1911] (*Methuen*). 1911.

The Card : A Story of Adventure in the Five Towns (*Methuen*). 1911.

Hilda Lessways (*Methuen*). 1911. (Second vol. of the Clayhanger trilogy.)

The Feast of St Friend (*Hodder & Stoughton*). N.D. [1911].

The Matador of the Five Towns (*Methuen*). 1912. Translated into Esperanto, 1919.

Mental Efficiency, and other Hints to Men and Women [an expanded edition of " The Reasonable Life " ; see above] (*Hodder & Stoughton*). 1912.

Milestones : A Play in Three Acts. By Edward Knoblauch and Arnold Bennett [first acted, 1912] (*Methuen*). 1912.

Those United States (*Secker*). 1912.

The Regent : A Five Towns Story of Adventure in London (*Methuen*). 1913.

The Plain Man and his Wife (*Hodder & Stoughton*). N.D. [1913]. Revised as Marriage (*Hodder*). 1916.

Paris Nights, and other Impressions of Places and People (*Hodder & Stoughton*). 1913.

The Great Adventure : A Play of Fancy in Four Acts [dramatic version of " Buried Alive " ; see above ; first acted, 1911] (*Methuen*). 1913.

Friendship and Happiness : A Plea for the Feast of St Friend (*Hodder & Stoughton*). N.D. [1914].

The Price of Love (*Methuen*). 1914.

Liberty : A Statement of the British Case (*Hodder & Stoughton*). 1914.

Over There. War Scenes on the Western Front (*Methuen*). 1915.

These Twain (*Methuen*). 1916. (Final vol. of the Clayhanger trilogy.)

The Lion's Share (*Cassell*). 1916.

Books and Persons (*Chatto & Windus*). 1917.

A National Responsibility. Future and Employment of the Disabled (*John Heywood*). 1917.

The Title : A Comedy in Three Acts [produced 1918] (*Chatto & Windus*). 1918.

ARNOLD BENNETT

The Pretty Lady (*Cassell*). 1918.

The Roll-Call (*Hutchinson*). 1918.

Self and Self-Management: Essays About Existing (*Hodder & Stoughton*). 1918.

Judith: A Play in Three Acts (*Chatto & Windus*). 1919.

Our Women. Chapters on the Sex-Discord (*Cassell*). 1920.

From the Log of the *Velsa* (*Chatto & Windus*). 1920. (Published in U.S.A. in 1914). Frontispiece by the Author.

Body and Soul: A Play in Four Acts (*Chatto & Windus*). 1922.

The Love Match: A Play in Five Scenes (*Chatto & Windus*). 1922.

Mr Proback (*Methuen*). 1922.

Things That Have Interested Me (*Chatto & Windus*). First series, 1921; second series, 1923.

How to Make the Best of Life (*Hodder & Stoughton*). 1923.

Riceyman Steps (*Cassell*). 1923.

Don Juan de Marana (*Privately Printed*). 1923.

PREFACES OR INTRODUCTIONS TO—

The Belmont Book, by Vados (*Smith, Elder*). 1911.

Marie Claire, by M. Audoux [translation] (*Chapman & Hall*). 1911.

Fecundity *versus* Civilisation, by Adelyne More (*G. Allen & Unwin*). 1916.

In the Royal Naval Air Service, by Harold Rosher (*Chatto & Windus*). 1916.

The Art of E. A. Rickards (*Technical Journals*). 1920.

ILLUSTRATIONS

A Floating House, by Cyril Ionides and J. B. Atkins (*Chatto & Windus*). 1918.

INDEX OF THE PRINCIPAL
REFERENCES